Esemplastic

Many and One

by Karian Markos

First Edition:
First printing

Cover design by Edward Rebek

ISBN-13: 979-8-9880919-4-3

Highland Park Poetry Press
1690 Midland Avenue
Highland Park, Illinois 60035

Esemplastic – Many and One

Karian Markos

For Daphne

Esemplastic – Many and One

Table of Contents

Karian Markos

Sunday

as a kid I wished for conformity

my name sounds like another word—
    what vultures call their breakfast
      Marion with a K
blaming my parents for their ignorance of English homophones is
unfair

their thoughtful creativity conceived of this mishmash
for fear a Spanish rooster would awkwardly crow my real name
on the first day of kindergarten—

    Kyriaki and kikiriki sound awfully similar

and so abrasive to small, third-generation German Irish ears
and quite the tongue twister for a teacher

the solution—

    Karian kicks six kittens quick
    Karian kicks six kittens quick
    Karian kicks six kittens quick

rolls off the tongue

my Greek name means Sunday so I could have been a Sunny—

    Sunny sells seashells by the seashore
    Sunny sells seashells by the seashore
    Sunny sells seashells by the seashore

just as easy and no animals were harmed

as a kid I wished for conformity
for sleepovers and dances with boys
for ham and cheese instead of spinach and feta
for time outs instead of flying shoes
for the freedom my ancestors coveted

the weight of my family tree was placed square on my shoulders
its reputation was secured in a vault between my legs
pride bedded shame and my tangle of dual loyalties was born

two flags   two homes   two names

Nostos

For the sailor and mother that stand watch on the shores of
Kardamyla, Chios, Greece

If not for the moon, night
would swallow the open sea
at the horizon. The captain
of the *Tahitis* waits to see
the flicker of the lighthouse,
sole along this coast to guide him,
before he turns to port.

The sky's velvet curtain
is pricked with longing and hope.
He knows the patterns—
how they change with the seasons.
The waters he navigates are unpredictable
and so he is mindful, cautious
not to run aground as he steers his ship

into the narrow, shallow-bottomed bay.
This sea has swallowed the dreams of many,
draping billowing, black sails over ships
and windows, sending widows
into its depths to follow.

Every woman in this village
has bowed over mixing bowls
and seasoned their food with salt
and bitter tears, whispering
nightmare omens into the east wind
to be carried away by the sunrise.

As he enters the bay, the lantern-dotted
mountainside sings of his homecoming.
A sentinel lamppost illuminates the jetty.
The path is narrow and the bay
only deep enough at the center
for his caïque to pass without running aground.

A bronze-hearted mother,
shading her eyes day and night,
gazes over the horizon.
No man here returns to an empty shore.

After docking his ship,
the captain greets the woman
with a tip of his hat and a courtly smile.
He ascends his marble plinth and turns north
toward the mouth of the bay. He takes hold
of his binoculars, straightens his shoulders,
whereupon he assumes his watch.

Legacy

I remember the hollow whoosh
through the hallways at night

sea sound echoes in dusty air
patrimony defaced by soundwaves

and pen strokes, peeling paint on
walls marked with arrogance

enough to flip ancestors' bones
in their steel, photo-marked boxes

the house stands empty
a crack splits face from foundation

none of us speak to the past
or to each other

Break Bread

we break bread with intent
to commune, to nourish
we split the loaf, its tender crumb revealed

we consume tradition and labor
fill our bellies with brotherhood—
          sweetening our blood
the thing broken mending our bonds
the thing broken making us whole again

Other

My ancestors left their homes cloaked in thick,
ethnic overcoats—a defined otherness.
Upon my creation, they convey to me a duality.

I am the bridge between lands and generations.
A recombinant being, unassimilated,
belonging to both and neither.

Cul de sac

The door to anywhere was here.

Our asphalt grew jasmine blossoms from apple seeds.
Our songs hung in the air at sunset.
Our feet made the footprints in the concrete.

We had nothing and everything
as we stumbled, shoulder to shoulder,
down the sidewalk where our dreams were born.

Prairie Tides

as cornflower blue an expanse as is the prairie sky
there is no prairie grass that can mimic my sea
no matter how hard I squint and imagine

no matter how light falls upon the Kentucky Blue
through what prism its color passes refracted onto my irises
it expresses itself in greens and browns

no matter the undulations of its blades
ebbing and flowing in howling wind
no matter how many dandelion tufts float along
its waves will never crest and break crowned in white

no matter how forgiving beneath my feet
I cannot dive into its springy dew
unless I shrink myself smaller than a droplet
        or wait until summer rains bring floodwaters
        enough to carry me to my beloved shore

One Urban Tree to Another

I admire you from across the avenue
as more grey-on-grey, uniform buildings
sprout from new foundations
You—the scrappy tree that persists through the development

Your gnarled trunk and roots cry rebellion
bust through the concrete designed to contain them
half your branches are missing and those that remain
grow at an angle that would have Pythagoras perplexed

spring has come and you are without leaves
indefatigable, you require no sustenance but determination
You should have toppled long ago but you're still here
flipping the bird to city trucks with vendettas
for infringing on power line sovereignty

You stand your ground, a symbol of defiance
I admire your resilience, your grit
You are a beacon of life
broken in body but not in spirit
against all odds and heavy machinery

Chimera

I dreamt an impossible dream
scribbled it on college-rule paper
folded the page and tucked it in my pocket
while I pursued more probable realities

the ink faded at the creases
the paper thinned where I fingered the page
rubbing the folds with nostalgia
as if a genie would spring out
to grant me this scrawled wish

it remains unfulfilled, abides
at the seams of the patchwork
person it created / the odd collection
of disjointed limbs that continues to add to itself
with hope to one day be complete

Beware the Art of Ego

the artist harvests poppies in June
partakes of mountainside haze
fluttering petals, speckles on new grass

crimson pointillist dots combine
form waves like silky fabrics in the breeze
they quiver beneath the stroke of an eager brush

she bows to the creative flow, a liminal deluge
eroding the soil around the ephemeral blooms
she uproots the image, filters it through her lens

conveys it into permanence, lays claim to title
landslide in the grassy foothills
proffers self at the value of story

The Mandarin's Dilemna

for the Mandarin to shed its peel
to discard its protective layer
and sit on a plate exposed
it would have to accept that it may be devoured
hungrily and unceremoniously

would it be too much
for the Mandarin to hope
that if it disrobes
undoes its pithy corset
revealing its segments
they would one by one

pass through a pair of delicately parted lips
perhaps grazing them gently
be laid onto a most appreciative tongue
and swirled and savored until
the thin skin containing its hundreds of juice sacs
bursts open in a flood of ecstasy

why else but for its trepidation
would it attempt to preserve itself
when the alternative is to rot
without having shared its gifts

Deliberate

a tired waltz beat
thumps in my head

watch, see me
a naked girl
you watch me be

fuzzy, flickering television static
flip, flip through the white sand

you call my name
the sound cracks through my brain
and I pause

the ground creeps away from my feet

I pluck a moment out of the air
stare at it squirming between my fingers

it withers
as I decide
what to do
what to do

Porcelain Girl

wait, wait, wait
I was told
patience, patience
I was taught patience
Good things, no—the best things
come to those who wait

the best things come to those who wait
I repeated, quoting my father's
misquote of the old adage, adapted for
common parlance by the Heinz corporation

My mother had a porcelain figurine
displayed in a curio cabinet
the doll had sculpted chestnut hair
glass eyes, soft-looking hands
and in all her years still
has never tasted a good ketchup

I emulated her poise, it felt natural,
as I sat opposite her, studying her
patiently waiting,
patiently

Cluck, Cluck

my whole life I've been a dog
barking up the wrong trees
baffled about what I could be doing wrong
that consistently resulted in fruitlessness

I only realized the truth
as I sat beneath a fruit laden tree
waiting for an apple to fall
into my mouth

The truth is—

I don't like apples
and I am not a dog

I am just a chicken

No, I won't be coming back to the office

this morning,
I will get ready for work
I will dress myself knowing
I will sweat through my suit
by nine-thirty or ten
even though I put on extra deodorant
with baby powder on top for absorption

around noon,
the fabric under my arms will be dry
I'll walk around the office
with white rings around my armpits
and everyone who sees me will notice
and whisper and giggle when I pass by
they'll think I have bad hygiene
I will be known around the water cooler
as the pretty brunette with the glandular problem

at lunchtime,
I will walk back to my desk
(after ten minutes in the bathroom
feverishly scrubbing deodorant residue)
I will take a plastic bag from my briefcase
(it will be filled with saltines)
and then I'll remember I didn't pour a cup of coffee
on my way back from the bathroom
and I'll get up again (or I will not
and sit and eat my crackers dry, regretting it
after they suck up all the juices in my mouth)

later on,
I will check my email ten times in one hour
and I will have nineteen texts from my real estate agent
she will have found me my dream home, again
and I will not answer if she calls me
at 4:56 I will look at the clock
at 4:57 I will look at the clock

at 4:57 I will look at the clock
at 4:58 I will look at the clock

at 4:59,
I will get up and put on my coat
I will walk five hundred thirty-four steps
then I'll be in the parking lot
twenty-six steps to the second floor
I will turn left and not find my car
then I will turn right and find it
where I thought I left it yesterday but didn't
I will have a slight flash of déjà vu
and I'll shake my head and take a breath

when I turn on my engine,
bachata music will blast from the radio
reggaeton y maaaaas
I will notice that I am on the second floor
I will get out of my car
(but before I do, I will turn up the music to max vol)
and I will climb onto the front hood
and stomp my heels into it like a flamenco dancer

I will laugh and twirl
and I will jovially throw myself over the ledge
into the guest parking lot below
I'll float down like a feather
and bounce off the pavement like a marshmallow
I will sing at the top of my lungs
and run as fast as I can back to where I started
and make different choices when I get there

Algos

I looked out through the incessant rain—
      nose pressed to glass
a little pond had formed under the canopy of a mopey cypress tree
where Freddy the gator sat waiting for me—
      steam rising from his nostrils
fear chewed at my intestines as I calculated which was worse—
      inside or out

Atomic Data

I am not a TikTok chattel
a series of labels
affixed to a profile

I am not a commodity
to be packaged and sold
my eye movements tracked

I am not a Dole banana
stickered, bundled, sprayed
to force the green out of my skin

I am more than a random sum
of interactions catalogued
and housed a neat box

I am. You are too.
Our aggregate power far exceeds
the value of their analytics.

Interrobang

I try my best with punctuation
though I, like Socrates,
am aware of the potential breadth
of my unknown unknowns.

I learned something new today
from a wordsmith's email
with subject line "interrobang"
and the thing was as I thought.

A suggestive sort of punctuation
to indicate rhetorical questions.
An exclamation point penetrating a question mark
with potential to denote other coital surprises.

I may never have occasion to use it.
A lady never kisses and tells.

ashes, ashes

we all fall down—
        eventually

in the meantime, I sometimes worry

I have half a question to ask before I yield to the moderator
    am I
    a drop
    a grain
    a scrap
    …?

I accept the fiat, but—

anxiety is wasteful, wasteful
and sometimes I waste my mind

Meditation

a flipped switch

tomorrow is gone

now is a barefaced eternity

  relapse—

I commit to thought

ignore the mantra

move beyond this interminable present

Flow

ideas surge, strike the concentration
a neuronal barrage, electric and chemical

they burn up like comets in the atmosphere
lost in the space between dendrite and hand

Apo-calypso

black out
ink runs down swollen cheeks
smacked with blush
artificial noses burn (crystals), no regrets—
bodies dance through sticky heat
and mosquito sickness
heaving, writhing
in the syncopate rhythm
of a down beaten drum
insides melt, the sweet syrup
pours over pancake-poor saps
in love-longing agony

lust lingers, logic empties
into boundless space filled with the sounds
of loud ringing nasty bells
that sear so, so sensitive ears
sweet psychosis chimes through
an otherwise silent symphony

blind nymphs spring from treetops
fall through the finite sky below
their immature wings snap
under the pressure of thick, putrid air
their tiny screams quickly fade

the people—worlds collide—continuous cries
tidal waves crash and pull them out to sea
so salty and wet, sweat polluted
bodies bloated buoyant, one atop the other
they slowly sink to the bottom
oceans filled to the banks but flooding still
gravity, graces drown in melancholy madness

no more happy faces
no traces of life in glazed blue gazes
out roll lolled tongues from listless mouths
voices stricken from the records recorded

parasites dance over death
suck the juicy eyeballs out of every open pair
through lock-jawed clenched teeth
wring the color from sea anemones
a dry white is left behind
tango-dipped backs arch deep
shrieks of orgasmic pleasure escape
meniscus-slime covered mouths
skeletons quiver
breaths quicken to match the tempo

Hope—overcome, exhausted—
sinks into the smoky atmosphere
quietly falls limp
through the hazy film separating
destruction
from the destroyed

and Death—inter(static) reigns

Seventeen Years Later

At twenty-one,
there's no way
I would have
worn a jacket
in this situation.

Now at thirty-eight
I find myself
waiting in line
outside a warehouse
in New York,
getting looked up

and down
by a doughier version
of Joey Fatone.
I could probably
break him in half
if I wanted to.
I do CrossFit now.

I've never been
into the club scene,
and I'm extra
not-into-it now.
But here I am,
shackled to the
vanity chain-gang

on my way to the
front of the line.
I suppose I'm not
that different from
any one of these
slightly post-pubescent
fun-suckers except that
I'm wearing a jacket.

I hadn't really cared
about appearances until
I downloaded Instagram.
I wonder which filter
hides middle-aged
dewy-eyed despondency.
Valencia? I check
my eyebrows in the window
to my right, smooth them
out with a couple of
swipes of my naked ring
finger. Pucker lips—Selfie!
Fuck.

I'm three pre-game
martinis in and
bored out of my wits.
I retreat to the mini
version of my therapist
who I've been paying
to occupy a cubicle
behind my right eye.
He's chatty.

A welcome diversion
from the stretchy pants
squeezing my thrice
post-partum belly.
The preemptive band-aids
I wrapped around my toes
are unfortunately squishing
their way through the adorable
peep at the front of my shoes,

though I'm not the only
train wreck here. A
silicone six walks through
the velvet gate and I
am next in line.

"I.D. miss?"
Miss? I'll take it.
Getting in the club.
Stretching the truth.

Summer's End

my summer is coming to an end
a smolder, skin barely a flush
desire's wily arms slacken and sag
the seat of creation shifts
from belly to mind

my summer is coming to an end
rose colored, it hangs low in the sky
cicadas decrescendo, bees prepare
for dearth, emptiness fills the vacancies
I am needed less, wanted less

my summer is coming to an end
my autumn is beginning
night chews the edges of day
mind skips the foreshortened winter
sees itself breach the horizon

my summer is coming to an end
a flicker in falling leaves
it kneels breathless at autumn's feet
begs a Monarch on a parallel path to extinction
to ferry her to timelessness on his velvet wings

Shades of Grass

a vow kept in faith
binds to one side, the
mind and spirit
> free to wonder, wander the mythical
> *land on the other side*
> where what ifs and
> daydreams roam in herds
> grazing upon greener grass
> to their heart's content

Our Agreement

our love is—
> a lingering dream
> a pair of hands upon tired shoulders
> a prayer for relief
> a will where there is none
> a codicil to revoke burden

Phantom

a *some color* sky hovers above us

you and I
breathe the same current

one faces right
one faces left

I leave an impression quickly swallowed
before a glimpse of my shadow
told you I had been lying there

(solidified)
my whisper crept behind your eyes
and constructed a vision so clear

you touch the space my words created
beneath an invisible blanket
I sleep soundly tucked under the same

Frailty of the Modern Ego

In general, words with x's bother me
Xanax, anxiolytics, Cinemax…
I'm not confident that they express
what's behind them consistently enough
to be truly meaningful in conversation.

For me, coffee and fruit always sound good in the morning.
A solid routine for a mother trying to mask an eating disorder
that has been around since it became obvious
that if one makes a mistake, it can be corrected most of the time.
So, no need for pills here.

Last week, I had a discussion with someone about benzodiazepines
while standing in the school parking lot.
It is my professional opinion that you can get arrested
for driving under the influence,
even if you aren't actually driving.
Its codified.
But a little action would make the drop-off line a lot more interesting.
So my personal advice would be different,
had I been asked to elaborate on the subject.

Which brings me to owls…

Owls are wise creatures
when discussing lollipops,
and how licking can get people places they want to go,
especially if they like being at the center of everything.

But otherwise,
owls can't be trusted to deliver sound advice.

The Plea

I feel it.
Mom, I feel *it*.
Help me
      Help me
            Help me please…
H
    Can I…
E
    How to…
L
    What can I…
P

do to (HELP ME)
help you defeat an enemy
that has swallowed
saber tooth tigers
and mammoths
in its black tar pit

If Andromeda Had Sung

a three-pronged prelude
a jealous reprise
chained to a refrain
save me, save me

an earthquake chord thrums
a slow crescendo
tsunami wave tempo
save me, save me

a modulation in response
a savior comes

chokes the pattern
kills the refrain

frees the songstress

Vespers

Every evening, as I ready myself for sleep,
I release a prayer into the night with the hope
a star is listening. An industrious and caring star
who will intercept it, take it to the
One Who Watches from the intermediate spaces,
and bolster my plea with an observation of its own.

Something like, "She really is lovely.
A warm-hearted person. Perhaps she deserves a break."

I imagine the One Who Watches will hear this
and grant my wish, a star being so much higher above
suspicion than a human. Perhaps he'll grant my appeal
knowing that stars are the finest judges of character.

The Note

"I am confined to a space the size of…"
Hm. A small melon? A large grapefruit?
I'm not positive—and there's no way
(at least that I know of) to precisely
measure the size of my cranial cavity
until the post-mortem.

Even then, procedures done out of curiosity
would be inappropriate (out of respect,
of course) so there would have to be questions
about the cause for an autopsy to be ordered.
I suppose (depending on the circumstances)

there might be a discrepancy between those findings
and what is accurate at this very moment. And
unless I say something now, the pathologist won't
know that it even mattered that I knew
what size fruit best described it.

Most likely, it would be too late to receive
a satisfactory answer to properly craft the verse.

Wings

I sprouted wings today
and rode aloft on a warm
gust of gratitude

life in panoramic view
gives me hope enough
to coast into tomorrow

All Things Justified

we are all guilty of selective blindness—

> I didn't see...
> I didn't hear...
> I didn't know...

so many of us spent our childhoods
pink-faced for some reason or another

> *the mouth on her*

> *he's a bad boy*

> *whack, break, slam*

we sublimate—
make funny videos about chanclas
and wooden spoons, laugh about flinching,
crack jokes on our way to the hospital

and if we continue to—

> see no evil
> hear no evil
> speak no evil

or slather that pig in lipstick

or coat it in sugar

it—the ignorance, the pain, the enduring affliction—
will eventually go away...

right?

Seagull Shaman

Knowing the
fish beneath
the waves hide

from her beak,
she prays for
forgiveness.

Reflex drives
her act of
contrition.

The Vine

my mother gave me a seed when I was young—
    I planted it in my garden

the soil was so fertile, nearly everything grew
she told me the vine born from it
would someday bear good fruit

it sprouted as she foretold
and eager to stretch its limbs, it grew—

I cared for the vine as it flourished
shaped it, pruned it—
it grew a thick base, strong and resilient

as it aged, it hardened
and I could no longer tame it
its long, tangled mass outgrew my care

there is no fruit, I said—
    wringing my fingers

patience, she said, let it go—

its roots are strong
the sun will shine
the rain will come
and you must accept
that you may not see fruit
until the vine is ready to bear it

Reverie

you lay curled upon yourself, swaddled in grey seafoam
crowned, bathed, rocked by moonlit tides
I beg you to stay with me but—
    your image is fading

I squeeze my eyes shut, cling to the cloudy dream
to the sound of your heartbeat
it speaks to me through its rhythmic wave-break—
    tells me to let you go

I too hear the sea in your heartbeat
you say, as you make your exit
though it is not my preference to stay—
    I have tired of this deafening sound

Without Voice or Name

please
       say something, anything
a cry, a whimper even

My tattered eyes, contorted face reflect
on an empty gold plate on a granite wall.
How can I keep you alive, in absentia,

when you have no name to engrave.
I cannot accept limbo as an answer
for how you will spend eternity.

A candle flame burns, flickers,
drips wax onto my trembling fingers,
as I devise a way to contain
this malignancy of feeling.

A Compromise in Memoriam

the one known victory over death / memorialized
in a liturgical hymn / reminded me as I listened

to the resonant chant / that it was not your victory
you would need a champion at heaven's gate

I wished it was me painted beside you in memoriam
an icon of orthodoxy resting on immortal laurels

but I also understood loneliness and its afflictions
and therefore decided to compromise

I only let part of me die with you
the rest of me could tend to the living

The Race

whiplash flag billows crimson in the wind / crushed
    geraniums bleed onto slick cobblestones

dirt scattered amidst shards of crushed clay pots
    left too close to the roadside / the ground quivers

beneath bare pigeon-toed feet / rumbling of hightailed hooves fades
    you walk onto the road without looking

one wet-nosed straggler with mad eyes glowing remains / on his
approach
    the clapping fades / horror washes over the crowd

be careful they said / you cannot outrun the bull

To the Winds

a chant on the Mistral wind grounds my Icarus dove
shadows stretch long on the backs of a sea of flickering prayers

the midnight Bora turns flaming wicks to glowing embers
grey swirls curl wave over wave, vanish into the darkness

a brief extinction, the flame rekindled by the Cape Doctor
her wings revive, his resurrection song gusting warm beneath her

the Maestro conducts her graceful course by the light of the moon
uplifting, cradling her in the wisps of a rose scented cirrus headed for
dawn

Weapon of Choice

I drive my kids to school every day.
The quirky crossing guard on the
street corner is wearing a flamingo
hat today. He also has a knitted
octopus hat he wears on auspicious
occasions, like the last day before
spring break. You wouldn't expect

him to own a plethora of such items
by looking at his frowning demeanor,
but appearances can be deceiving.
I wear black on most days. Mainly
because I am mourning the loss of
my beach body despite my many
concerted efforts to save her. But also,

because I like it when things are the same
on the outside as they are on the inside.
Which brings me to this morning's murder.
Yes, I killed someone. I was headed to the gym
when a lady sounded a war horn from her car
and shot me with a double-birded f-bomb.
I may have accidentally cut her off on the train tracks.

I acknowledged the error of my ways,
though my honor was soiled.
So, I killed her.
I killed her with kindness. I feel no remorse,
having thus won many battles. It was for the best.

Expression of the Divine Alphabet

The divine alphabet
has three letters—

A I Ω

I am the self.

I am the animate.

I will depart the vessel
that briefly contains me.

I will scatter, become
particles and waves
suspended outside time,
leaving only A and Ω

where three and two are one.

Eternity

it rolls by, stops for no one, nothing
a self-propelled train on a double-looped track
we're born on board with a one-punch ticket
watch the pictures flicker by for a while
maybe leave a mark or divot on our seat
quick-like, before the conductor comes around again

Acknowledgments

I would like to thank *Bombfire, Living Crue Magazine, Prairie Light Review, Highland Park Poetry,* and the Illinois State Poetry Society for publishing or awarding versions the following poems:

"Sunday." *Living Crue Magazine,* Vol. 2.

"Nostos." *Prairie Light Review,* Spring 2022.

"Frailty of the Modern Ego." 2019. *Bombfire,* www.bombfirelit.com.

"Break Bread." *Odes: Poets Praising People, Places and Things,* edited by Mary Beth Bretzlauf & Jennifer Dotson, Highland Park Poetry, 2022, p. 22.

"Reverie." *Distilled Lives,* Volume 6, Illinois State Poetry Society, 2022.

"Seagull Shaman." 2nd Place, Highland Park Poetry Award, Illinois State Poetry Society Contest, 2022.

"The Mandarin's Dilemma." *Prairie Light Review,* Spring 2022.

"The Vine." *Prairie Light Review,* Spring 2023.

Many thanks to Lennart Lundh for selecting this book for the Prairie State Poetry Prize for First or Second Book. Thank you, Jennifer Dotson of Highland Park Poetry Press for your magnificent effort and support in bringing this book to fruition. Thank you, Ed Rebek for lending me your talent and expertise in designing the cover image. Thank you to my husband, Dr. Michael Markos, and my children, Fania, Mairi, and Marcella, for your love, support, and inspiration. My golden thread leads back to you. Thank you to my parents, George and Mary Karavolos for nurturing the seed of creativity in me. Thank you to my family and friends for your loving support. Many thanks to Mardelle, Lee, Abby, Carole, Kathryn, Mary Beth, Mary Lynn, Mary Jane, and Susan for your insight and comments on the many versions of the poems contained in this book. Thank you, Mary Biddinger for everything you taught me all those years ago. Thank you, George Makrinos for your uplifting words. Thank you, Maria Karamitsos for your longstanding support of my creative endeavors, and for your efforts to shine a spotlight on artists in the Greek community."

About the Author

Karian Markos is a Greek American poet, fiction writer and nonprofit attorney living with her husband and three children in the western suburbs of Chicago, Illinois. Her award-winning work has been published in magazines and anthologies such as *Living Crue Magazine, Highland Park Poetry, Prairie Light Review, Bombfire* and elsewhere. Please visit www.karianmarkos.com for more information and updates.

***

Karian Markos' *Esemplastic – Many and One* is the winner of Highland Park Poetry's 2024 Prairie State Poetry Prize for a 1st or 2nd Book. The judge for this year's contest was Chicago poet Lennart Lundh.

Karian Markos

Made in the USA
Monee, IL
03 July 2024

60852682R00039